the
BUCKET
LIST
book

the BUCKET LIST book

500 things

you really should do

ELISE DE RIJCK

BATSFORD

Hi, my name's Elise, nice to 'meet' you!

A few weeks before my 29th birthday I started to panic. It was the fear of turning 30. I suddenly realised that life is going by so fast it's time to do the things I have always wanted to now, rather than put them off until tomorrow.

That's why I made a list of 30 things that I still want to do before my 30th birthday. Writing a book is just one of them, and here it is, right in front of you. I would like THE BUCKET LIST BOOK to inspire and motivate you, to make as many of your dreams come true as possible. But that's enough about me, this is your book! Enjoy it and may all your dreams come true!

This book will change your life. Honestly. But don't panic, it isn't a self-help book and you won't be overwhelmed by life's great philosophical questions. This book will make you dance in the rain, it will encourage you to climb trees, save lives and see the world. It will make you smarter and with a bit of luck, you will become very fit and fulfil all your dreams at the same time.

I admit that this might not be <u>entirely</u> true. You are the only person who can realise your dreams! But it will give you a helping hand. We all have dreams we can't fulfil because of our hectic lives. They are the things we say we will do later because we are too busy now. But what if 'later' is now? (Oops, a philosophical life question.) Let's delete words like 'later' and 'if' from our vocabularies and live for today. This book will give you 500 ideas to set you on the path towards a more enriched life.

I challenge you to do everything, or those things you want to do, because it is your life. There are no rules of the game and no time limits attached. After page 168 you will find pages for your personal goals and where you can design your own perfect life. They include five tips to help you draw up the perfect bucket list.

Are you ready for new adventures? Ready, steady, go!

Share your experiences on Instagram, Facebook or Twitter with the hashtag #abucketlistlife. You could post a motivational quote, a selfie taken on one of the book's challenges, or a photo of the tropical island you had always wanted to visit.

Stop dreaming,
start doing!

today is the
YOUNGEST
you'll ever be.
SO IF NOT NOW, WHEN ...

1. ☑ Make a bucket list. Congratulations, you have ticked off your first entry. Keep it up!

2. ☐ TAKE A DOG FOR A WALK. OR A CAT, A RABBIT OR A GOLDFISH.
If you manage to do the latter, I would like to see the evidence! #abucketlistlife

☐ Write a love letter or ☐ receive one. **3.**
To........................./ From.....................

Love you
X forever

4. ☐ DANCE IN THE RAIN.
Like nobody's watching!

5. ☐ Go to a gig by _____
(Fill in your favourite artist/band.)

☐ And stand in the mosh pit.

6. ☐ HAVE A FOOD FIGHT.
IF YOU PREFER TO KEEP THE KITCHEN TIDY, HAVE ☐ A SNOWBALL FIGHT ☐ A WATER FIGHT, OR ☐ A MUD FIGHT, BECAUSE THEY ARE JUST AS GOOD. BUT IF YOU AREN'T QUITE THAT BRAVE, ☐ A PILLOW FIGHT WOULD DO JUST AS WELL.

7. ☐ Stand on stage and ☐ receive a standing ovation.
Applause, please!

8. ☐ Go for a ride on a tandem.

9. ☐ Build a fire.
Outdoors! You don't want your home to go up in smoke!

10. ☐ Visit 10 capital cities, because you're so cosmopolitan!

☐ _ _ _ _ _ _ _ _ _ _ _ _ _ _   ☐ _ _ _ _ _ _ _ _ _ _ _ _ _ _

☐ _ _ _ _ _ _ _ _ _ _ _ _ _ _   ☐ _ _ _ _ _ _ _ _ _ _ _ _ _ _

☐ _ _ _ _ _ _ _ _ _ _ _ _ _ _   ☐ _ _ _ _ _ _ _ _ _ _ _ _ _ _

☐ _ _ _ _ _ _ _ _ _ _ _ _ _ _   ☐ _ _ _ _ _ _ _ _ _ _ _ _ _ _

☐ _ _ _ _ _ _ _ _ _ _ _ _ _ _   ☐ _ _ _ _ _ _ _ _ _ _ _ _ _ _

11. ☐ Conquer your greatest fear:

_ _

You're not chicken, are you?!

12. ☐ SING 'TEN GREEN BOTTLES' FOR 3 HOURS.

And now this song is stuck in your head for 3 days. Sorry!

☐ Walk barefoot through some grass. **13.**

Watch out for the dog poo!

☐ PULL OUT YOUR FIRST GREY HAIR.
YOU'RE STILL .... YEARS YOUNG!

14.

↗

(YES, YOU'VE SPOTTED IT: THIS IS WHERE YOU CAN GLUE THAT GREY HAIR; YUCK!)

15. ☐ GO ON A BLIND DATE. (YOU'RE STRONGLY ADVISED
AGAINST DOING SO IF YOU'RE IN A RELATIONSHIP!)

16. ☐ BINGE ON _____ (FOOD).

Highly recommended: sweets, chocolate or popcorn.
Seriously discouraged: chilli peppers (oh, the day
after) and garlic, especially if you're still going
on your blind date.

17. ☐ See ☐ your grandchildren grow up.

But first become a ☐ mummy ☐ daddy. **18.**

Congratulations!

19.

☐ Rescue a (human) being. Exciting, isn't it! How does it feel to be a hero?

20.

☐ Give blood (in which
case you may also tick 19) **21.**

Write a letter to yourself 10 years in the future ☐

- ->

☐ Help a homeless person. **22.**
Your heart is in the right place!

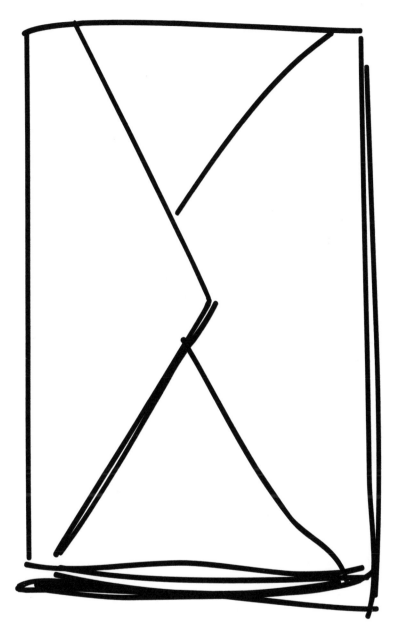

21. This is where you should stick the letter to your future self, in a sealed envelope. You must not open it before ... / ... / 20... . Can you hold back your curiosity for 10 years?

23. ☐ Visit Venice before it sinks ☐ and take a gondola ride.

☐ Write a book entitled: **24.**

----

25. ☐ Milk a cow! Moo!

☐ Go to a school reunion. (Take the initiative.)
☐ I would not have expected this person to become what
he/she is today: ---------------------------------- **26.**
I hardly recognised this person: ---------------------------
I would have preferred not to see this person again: ------------------- No one's reading this!

27. ☐ Throw a cake in somebody's face.
It was a ------------------ cake. Yummy!

28.
☐ Go skiing or ☐ snowboarding ☐ without breaking any bones.

29.
☐ Get super-fit. (You will thank yourself.)

30. ■ Sleep under the stars. Twinkle, twinkle.

Where? _____

Who with? _____

31. ■ Grow a moustache.

No ladies, not you!

32. ■ Spot a UFO ■ without worrying people will think you're mad.

33. ■ Visit all the continents:

- ■ Asia
- ■ Africa
- ■ North America
- ■ South America

- ■ Antarctica
- ■ Europe
- ■ Oceania

34.

■ Live (survive) one week without social media.

#digitaldetox #unplugging #signoff #disconnecttoreconnect

#welcometotheflipside #intotherealworld

35. ☐ Learn 10 new words (and use them).

☐ _____ ☐ _____
☐ _____ ☐ _____
☐ _____ ☐ _____
☐ _____ ☐ _____
☐ _____ ☐ _____

Oh you smartypants!

36. ☐ Do something incredibly brave. Tell us more:

_____

_____

_____

_____

_____

_____

_____

_____

*when was the last time
you did something for
the first time?*

_____

☐ Play bingo in a care home and ☐ call a false 'bingo'. **37.**

38. □ Wrap a snake around your neck.

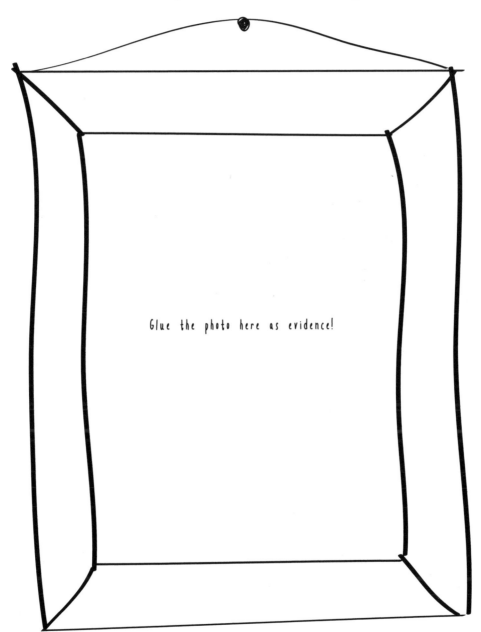

Glue the photo here as evidence!

39.

☐ Choose a favourite song. La la la la la la la la… What did you go for?

_____

_____

_____

40.

☐ Mow the lawn and enjoy the smell of freshly cut grass.

41.

☐ Jump into the swimming pool fully clothed or ☐ take a shower in your socks.

42.

☐ Go to an auction and ☐ put in a bid. Was your bid the highest? Yes/no.

43.

☐ Buy a house/apartment.

44.

☐ Take part in a game show on TV.
☐ The local pub quiz also counts, if you're shy!

45. ☐ Inspire somebody. Who and how?

_____

_____

_____

_____

_____

_____

_____

_____

_____

_____

_____

_____

_____

46. 💍 Marry the love of your life.

Stick a photo of your perfect day here!

.... / .... / 20....

47. ☐ Experience world peace.

Wouldn't we all love to ...

48. ☐ REGISTER AS AN ORGAN DONOR.

Another heroic thing you can do!

49. ☐ WATCH A FIREWORK DISPLAY.

50. ☐ Send a message in a bottle.

Include your address - someone might reply.
you never know.

51.

☐ Bet everything on red in a casino.

☐ Ask for a pay rise.
(Particularly if the ball landed on black.)

53. ☐ Sing to an audience. Karaoke counts!

First you'll be afraid, you will be petrified
You'll keep thinkin' you could never sing this song with pride
But then you'll spend so many nights thinking how it could go wrong,
and you grew strong, you learned how to sing a song.
You will not crumble! You will not lay down and die!
Oh no not you! You will survive! Hey hey!

54. ☐ Get into the Guinness Book of World Records.
How?

□ BE HAPPY.

55

56. ☐ Be an uninvited guest at a party ☐ or try to get into a sold-out performance.

57. ☐ Sit in the driver's or passenger seat in a convertible and sing along to the worst song at the top of your voice. Boom boom boom boom!

58. ✶ Make a wish when you see a shooting star.

59. ☐ Fire a bullet.

At the shooting gallery at the fair, of course!

60. ☐ Win a (cash) prize. What/how much have you won?

_____

61.

☐ Touch your nose with your toes. Yay!

62.

☐ Make friends with someone from a different culture.

63.

☐ Smoke a cigar ☐ in Cuba.

64. ☐ GET YOUR DRIVING LICENCE. VROOM, VROOM!

65. ☐ CLIMB A TREE.

66. ☐ Find a four-leaf clover. ❧

67. ☐ Taste wine of the same vintage as you. The year was ....

68.

☐ Think of an April Fool's Day prank and play it on somebody.

Tell us more:

_____

_____

_____

_____

_____

Ha ha, that's funny!

69.

☐ Put your name into Google.

How many hits? _____

70.

☐ Kiss a frog and see if it turns into a prince. Mwah!

71.

☐ Think of a word and make others use it.
The word is: _____
and means: _____

Why don't you think 'fossie' is a word? It is now.
You are a fossie*!

☐ Use chopsticks ☐ in China. **72.**

73. ☐ Book room service in a hotel.

74. ☐ Spend 24 hours on your own.

* A fossie is someone who wants to live life to the max every day.

☐ Spy on somebody (in disguise).
Who? _____
Did they notice you?
Yes/no.

75.

76. ☐ Dance the Macarena. Hey, Macarena!

77.

☐ Adopt a pet.
Is it a tiger? A monkey? A giraffe?
Or did you go for a cat or dog in the end?
Called _____
woof/meow!

78. ☐ DIVE INTO ICY COLD WATER. BRRRR.

79. ☐ Stay in bed all day.

80. ☐ Disguise your voice when you answer the phone and keep pretending it's a wrong number (even if they have already realised it's you).

Who's calling? Hello, helloooo?

81. ☐ Walk on hot coals. Ouch!

Put a photo of your really hot adventure here!

82. ⬜ Dye your hair and discover what it's like to be a brunette/blonde.

BEFORE:

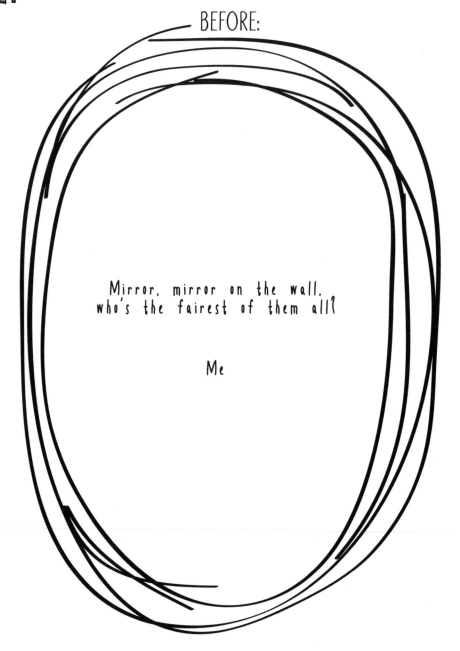

Mirror, mirror on the wall,
who's the fairest of them all?

Me

AFTER:

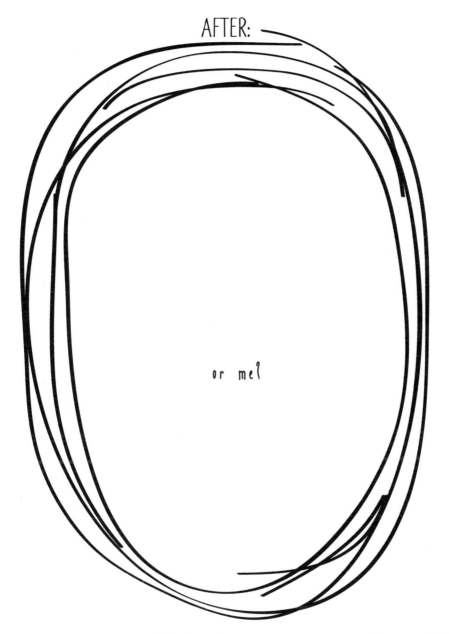

or me?

Well? Do blondes have more fun? Yes/no. Or were you smarter as a brunette? Yes/no.

83. ☐ Stand on a mountain top.

It doesn't have to be Mount Everest!

84. ☐ Fart in a lift.
(And pretend someone
else did it, of course.)

☐ Find the job of your dreams. **85.**

86. ☐ Stick to your New Year's resolution for at least a year.
Go on, tell us what it is. What have you decided to give up/
do this year?

_____ _____

_____

_____

87. ☐ Go backstage at a concert by

_____

34

collect
MOMENTS,
NOT THINGS.
Have STORIES
TO TELL, NOT
STUFF TO SHOW.

88. Ha Ha Ha Ha Ha
Ha ☐ Have hysterics ☐ at an inappropriate momen
Ha Ha Ha Ha Ha Ha

☐ Hug a tree. 89.

And don't ask why I've included this.

90. ☐ Make a complete fool of yourself.
(Maybe while you're hugging that tree?)

☐ Buy that really expensive item that has been 91.
on your wish list for ages. Because you are worth it!
What's on your wish list?

_____

_____

_____

_____ _____

92. ☐ Plant a tree ☐ and watch it grow.

93. ☐ Pretend you're someone else for an evening.
Have you always wanted to find out what it is like to come from Paris?
Today you're a Parisian!
C'est chic!

94.

☐ Turn upside down in a rollercoaster.

95.

☐ Sit on the back of a: ☐ horse
☐ cow
☐ bull
☐ donkey
☐ elephant.

96. ☐ HAVE A RIDE IN A LIMOUSINE
☐ AND A GLASS OF CHAMPAGNE, OF COURSE!

97. ☐ VISIT (AT LEAST) 3 NATIONAL PARKS:

98.
☐ Become an expert at something.
What did you choose?

Every expert started out as a beginner.

99. ☐ Spot a wild animal, in the wild.

100. ☐ Write a song for somebody. Or better still:
☐ Ask someone to write a song for you!

101. ☐ SIT ON A MECHANICAL BULL
FOR AT LEAST 7 SECONDS.

102.
☐ Give someone a fright.

103. ☐ HAVE A SHOWER UNDER A WATERFALL
OR ☐ IN THE RAIN.

104.

☐ Write your name (and your beloved's) on a tree.

Retro-romanticism!

☐ Order 5 (!) scoops of ice cream all in one go from the ice-cream van. What are your top 5 flavours?

105.

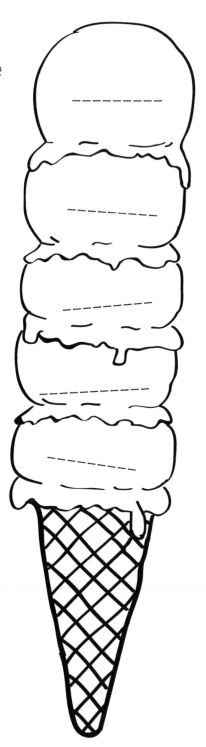

106.

☐ Play Cupid and introduce two people to one another.

Who?

_____ & _____

Did their relationship work out? Yes/no.

107.

☐ Take part in a first aid course or assemble a ☐ first aid kit to use at home. **Safety first!**

108. ☐ Fall in love.

109.

☐ Learn a new language. Which one did you choose?

Translate this sentence: my name is blah* and I'm a sweet little rabbit with a tiny fly on my nose.

*Fill in your own name.

110.

☐ Play at least one song on an instrument.

Feel funky. feel good. You've got the music in yoooou!

111.
- ☐ Swim in any of these oceans. Splish, splash!
- ☐ North Pacific
- ☐ South Pacific
- ☐ North Atlantic
- ☐ Indian Ocean
- ☐ Southern Ocean
- ☐ Arctic Ocean

112.

☐ Scuba dive or ☐ snorkel if you don't like to go below sea level.

113.
☐ Experience an earthquake.
Hopefully only a small one!

114.

☐ Travel first class.

115.

Have some ☐ professional
photos taken of you ☐ naked.
#abucketlistlife > if you dare!

116.

☐ Dance the tango
☐ in Buenos Aires.

117.

☐ Have your fortune told. What did the fortune-teller predict?

Do you think it will really happen? Yes/no.

118. ☐ PRINT OFF YOUR DIGITAL PHOTOS
BEFORE YOUR COMPUTER GIVES UP THE GHOST.

Thank me later.

119. See a rainbow ☐
☐ or make one.

120. ☐ WEAR A BLINDFOLD
FOR 24 HOURS. (NO CHEATING!)

(Stick a photo here.)

121. ☐ Wear odd socks. Unless you already do!

122.

☐ Make a will. What's going to happen to your stamp collection when you're no longer around?

_____
_____
_____ __
_____
_____ ____
_____
_____
_____
_____
_____
_____ _____
_____
_____ _____
_____
_____
_____
_____
_____ _____
_____
_____ _____
_____
_____ _____
. _____

This is the will of_____ drawn up on__/__/20__

Date / /

Registration number

country code

This is not a parking ticket because I am not authorised to issue them. But if I were, I'd give you two! Perhaps you're a little short-sighted or a superhero who's been called out suddenly on a life-saving mission. I am sure that parking here was not an act of selfishness, stupidity or inability on your part. Perhaps my lack of awareness of Park Like An Idiot Day is to blame!

Have a great day but maybe take
the bus tomorrow!
Best wishes,
A fellow road user

124. ☐ Learn how to tie a tie.

125. ☐ Give a lift to a hitchhiker.

126. ☐ Build a raft ☐ and sail for
at least 100 metres.

127.

☐ Dance on the table.

If the cat's away.

128.

☐ Play hide-and-seek in a public place.
Where? _____

☐ > 7 You can do better than that, try again.

☐ > 7-15 Well done, try to find more friends to make it really exciting!

☐ > 15-30 Isn't this great?

☐ 30+ Fantastic!

☐ 100+ Wow, what a trouper!

129.

☐ Look up at the clouds and see shapes in them.

130.

☐ Throw money in a lucky fountain.
Now make a wish!

131.

☐ Go on holiday on your own. Do you dare? Where will you go to?

The world is a book, and those who do not travel read only one page.

132. ☐ Get a diploma. Or 2, or 3!

There's no such thing as too much education!

☐ Celebrate St Patrick's Day ☐ in Ireland.

133.

134.

☐ Change a baby's nappy.

135. ☐ HAVE A RIDE IN THE CAR OF YOUR DREAMS. (EVEN IF IT'S ONLY A TEST DRIVE.)

136. ☐ Tread grapes barefoot.

137. ☐ Float in the Dead Sea. How long did you float? ... hour(s) ... minute(s) ... second(s).

138. ☐ Get to know your neighbours. Do you know the saying about a good neighbour and a distant friend?

139. ☐ Visit the opera. What did you go and see?

_____

↗

Stick your opera ticket here.

140. ☐ Run a marathon.

Run, Forrest, run!

141. ☐ Read one of Shakespeare's plays. Which one did you read?

_____

☐ Go for a professional massage. **142.**
Enjoy it!

143. ☐ Eat an insect. Which one did you choose?

_____

144.

☐ Visit an ☐ active volcano. Which one?

_____ _____

145. ☐ Pretend you are a tourist in your own town
☐ and send someone a postcard.

☐ Learn to juggle with 3 balls. **146.**

147. ☐ Write a letter to 5 people who have had a
positive influence on your life.

1. _____
2. _____
3. _____
4. _____
5. _____

148. ☒ Get drunk.

149.

☐ Support a good cause. Which good cause and what is your role?

------------------------------------ -----

------------------------------ ------------

----

150. ☐ Fly (in) a helicopter.

☐ Swim naked. Did anyone see you? Yes/no.

151.

there are
SEVEN DAYS
IN A WEEK &
SOMEDAY
ISN'T ONE OF THEM

152. ☐ Write a poem.

Release the poet
in you!

153. ☐ Drink straight from the
beer tap in a pub. Cheers!

154. ☐ Attend a wedding party. Whose?

_____ & _____

155. ☐ Visit a museum and become really interested.
Which museum did you visit?

_____

☐ Sail a boat. **156.**

157.

☐ Get in touch again with a friend you haven't seen for years ☐ and go for a drink together. Who is it?

_____

158. ☐ Don't eat meat for a month.

159. ☐ Book a table in a restaurant under a silly name, such as Mr Britney Spears or Mrs Izit Good?

Make sure you turn up!

Which name did you use?

_____

☐ Inhale helium **160.** from a balloon.

161. ☐ Write down all your regrets and then forget about them by burning this piece of paper (not the entire book!).

_____

_____

_____

_____ _____

_____

_____

_____

_____

_____

_____

_____

_____

_____

_____

_____

Better an oops
_____

than a what if!

BURN BABY BURN

162. ☐ Don't ask for a plastic bag in the supermarket for at least a month.

163. ☐ THROW TOMATOES DURING THE LA TOMATINA FESTIVAL IN SPAIN.
☐ OR ORGANISE YOUR OWN MINI VERSION WITH FRIENDS.

164. ☐ TEST VIAGRA
☐ OR THE FEMALE LIBIDO ENHANCER PILL. (AVAILABLE SINCE 2016!)

165. ☐ Toss a pancake in the air ☐ and catch it.

166. ☐ Do an IQ test.

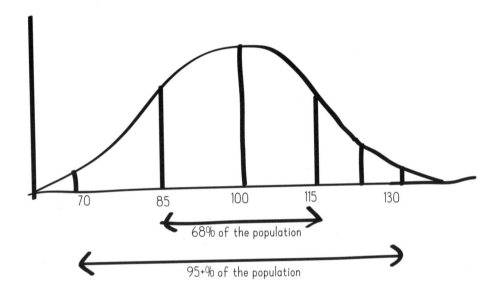

70   85   100   115   130

68% of the population

95+% of the population

Colour in your IQ in the diagram!

167.

☐ Swap your life with someone for one day.

Who did you choose? _____

What kind of things did you do?

-- ---

----------------------------- --------------

---------------------- --------------------

168.

BE HAPPY ABOUT WHO YOU ARE AND WHAT YOU LOOK LIKE.

169. ☐ Keep silent for 24 hours. Shush!

You're allowed to write notes.

170.

☐ Start a (useless) collection and don't stop until you have collected 100 items (suggestions include wine, postage stamps, posters of Justin Bieber …).
What did you collect?

----

171. ☐ Have a deep and meaningful conversation with a random stranger.

172. ☐ Put one foot on the moon.

173. ☐ SIT ON SOMEONE'S SHOULDERS DURING A GIG.

WHICH ONE? _

174. ☐ Go to the sauna.
Phew!

175.
☐ Swim in the rain.

176. ☐ Sit in a hot tub (outdoors)
while it's snowing.

177. ☐ Go and see a musical (live).

178. ☐ SIT ROUND THE CAMPFIRE AND ☐ TOAST MARSHMALLOWS.

179. ☐ Sign the petition against/for

- -

180. ☐ WALK UNDER A LADDER ON FRIDAY THE 13TH. UH OH! ☐ AND SEE A BLACK CAT. PHEW!

181. ☐ Put a mint in a glass of cola and watch it fizz!

182. ☐ Make a family tree.

183. ☐ Drop something silly in your friend's shopping trolley ☐ and film their response. Were you caught? Yes/no.

184. ☐ Play Monopoly with real money.

185. ☐ Go bowling ☐ and bowl a strike.

186.

☐ Help someone make a wish come true.
Whose did you choose? _____
And what was their wish?

_____

_____

_____

_____

187. ☐ Have breakfast served in bed.

But what about all those annoying crumbs?

188.

■ Become a member
of the 'Mile High Club'.

189.

■ Make a video of a typical day in
your life and watch it in 10 years' time.

190.

■ Let a snowflake
land on your tongue.

191.

■ Hand in your notice.
Note: only do this if you
don't enjoy your job!

192. ☐ Learn to whistle. Tweet tweet!

193.

☐ Invent something.
(A game, a recipe, an app or
maybe something even
bigger. Be ambitious!)

‑‑‑‑‑‑‑‑‑‑‑‑‑‑‑‑‑‑‑‑‑‑‑‑‑‑‑

‑‑‑‑‑‑‑‑‑‑‑‑‑‑‑‑‑‑‑‑‑‑‑‑‑‑‑

‑‑‑‑‑‑‑‑‑‑‑‑‑‑‑‑‑‑‑‑‑‑‑‑‑‑‑

‑‑‑‑‑‑‑‑‑‑‑‑‑‑‑‑‑‑‑‑‑‑‑‑‑

194. ☐ Motivate a friend to draw up a bucket list.
Better still: ☐ persuade someone to buy this book.
*wink*wink*

195. ☐ Experience a white Christmas.
Let it snow, let it snow, let it snow!

196. ☐ Have a posh picnic.
(I don't mean a sandwich in a park.)

☐ Dine by candlelight. Wow, how romantic! **197.**

198. ☐ Ask someone to give you a nickname ☐ or adopt one.
(But maybe that's a bit sad?)
What's your nickname? _____

☐ Use a meter to measure the loudness of **199.**
your scream in decibels.
So, how loud was it? ____DB
Loud enough for the Guinness Book
of World Records?
(See number 54).

200. ☐ Get your name in the newspaper.

↗

(Stick the article here.)

201.
☐ FIRST ORDER A DESSERT, THEN A MAIN COURSE, AND THEN A STARTER IN A RESTAURANT. JUST BECAUSE YOU CAN!

202.
☐ Kiss someone at the foot of the Eiffel Tower.

Who? _____

203.
◌ CRY WHILE WATCHING A FILM OR ◌ READING A BOOK.

204.
☐ Go to the toilet at a festival.

Because we all love doing it!

205.

☐ Go to the airport without knowing your destination. Where did you go?

_____

206. ☐ Don't watch television for a week. What did you do in the evenings?

_____

_____

_____

_____

_____

_____

_____

207. ☐ Celebrate Valentine's Day.

208. ☐ Go camping or ☐ glamping.

209. ☐ Don't look in the mirror for a whole day (not even on the sly.) Cover all the mirrors the night before!

210. ☐ Go on a double date. It makes love twice as beautiful!

211. ☐ Lose your way in a foreign country.

?????

←•→

212. ☐ Tell a tequila story.

(everyone has a tequila story!)

----

213. ☐ Ask someone out.

214. ☐ Allow yourself to be hypnotised and conclude that it did not work for you.

☐ Forgive someone for something they have done. **215.**

216. ☐ Find a pearl in an oyster.

☐ Trip over in public. On your face! **217.**

218. ☐ Draw on somebody's face while they're asleep.

This is a classic!

219. ☐ Feed ducks in a park.

☐ Clear the inbox in your email account and unsubscribe from all the newsletters you don't read anyway. **220.**

221. ☐ Make a beard from bath foam.

222.

☐ Do 'it' in public ☐ without

Naughty, naughty! being seen.

223.

☐ Count all your freckles and moles. There are _____

224.

☐ Sing a serenade to someone from a balcony.

225.

☐ CELEBRATE YOUR 50TH BIRTHDAY. HIP, HIP, HOORAY!

226.

☐ Build a snowman.

227.

☐ Break a bone. Was it your ☐ leg, ☐ arm, ☐ shoulder or ☐ something else?

_____

228. ☐ LOSE A SHOE AT A BALL.

229. ☐ Hail a cab in New York.

230. ☐
Go on a pub crawl.
Have fun!

231. ☐ Have a tattoo
(or don't).

232.
☐ DANCE THROUGH THE NIGHT UNTIL DAWN.

233.
☐ BOUNCE ON A TRAMPOLINE. HIGHER, HIGHER, HIGHER!

234.
☐ Paddle a canoe or kayak.

235.

☐ Visit a casino in Las Vegas.

236.

And now you're there, you
might as well get married
in the Little White Chapel.

237.

☐ Say it with flowers.
Who would/did you send them to? _____
What did you want to say?

_____

_____

_____

238. ☐ Ask a street artist to draw a caricature of you on this page!

239.

☐ Find out what really makes you happy:

_____

_____

_____

_____

_____

_____

_____

_____

240.

☐ Have dinner in a Michelin-starred restaurant. Which one? _____
Colour in the number of stars.

241. ☐ Visit a pyramid.

242.

☐ Learn how to swim. (Otherwise, you'll drown!)

243.

☐ Stop smoking, or, even better:
☐ never start.

244.

☐ Attend a tea ceremony
☐ in Japan.

245. ☐ Be lovesick.

It may seem like the end of the world, but don't forget: it will end. Soon enough you won't remember what you ever saw in him/her, I promise!

246. ☐ Get taped to a wall.

Do something mad!

247. ☐ STAND FACE TO FACE WITH THE
MONA LISA.

248. ☐ Stay overnight in
an ice hotel. Ice, ice baby!

249. ☐ Solve a Rubik's cube.

250. ☐ Visit Stonehenge
☐ and try to push over
a stone.

251. ☐ Go to a Cirque du Soleil performance.

252.

☐ Swim with dolphins. If that's too much of a cliché for you, try ☐ sharks or ☐ turtles.

253.

☐ Celebrate Christmas on the beach.

Will Father Christmas be wearing shorts or speedos? Something (or perhaps not very much) to consider!

254.

☐ Travel around the world.

255.

□ Cross the equator.

_____

10...
9...
8...
7...
6...
5...
4... 3...2...1!

256.

☐ Bet on the winning horse at the races.

257.

☐ Stop the Tower of Pisa from falling over. (You know what I mean, you've seen the tourist photos.)

258.

☐ Spend New Year's Eve in another country. Where? _____

259.

☐ Make a speech ☐ at a wedding.
List everything you said.

_____
_____
_____
_____
_____
_____
_____
_____
_____
_____

260.

☐ Go on a cruise.
(That's why you should learn
to swim — see number 242.)

261. ☐ Go on safari in Africa.

262. ☐ Enjoy carnival time in Rio de Janeiro. Tada-tada-tada-tada, Brazil!

263.

☐ Watch a film outdoors.
Or, better still:
☐ go to a drive-in cinema.

264. ☐ Drink beer at the Oktoberfest in Munich.

265.

☐ Go on a trip in a hot-air balloon.

Please don't throw anything over the edge!

(Stick a photo here of a breathtaking view.)

266. ☐ Make a call from a ☐ London telephone box.

LONDON CALLING

267.

☐ Say farewell to somebody you're really fond of.

This is not the happiest item in this
list, but sadly, it's part of life!
All the best!

268. ☐ Ride a motorbike, or ride pillion.

269. ☐ Be thirsty in the desert
☐ but luckily you have a drink with you.
Phew!

270. ☐ See the Northern Lights.

271.

☐ Watch a solar eclipse.

272.

■ Watch a lunar eclipse.

273.

☐ Make a list of all the people you love and tell them (no, not that you have made a list, but that you love them!)

274.

☐ Stand on the Grand Canyon Skywalk.

275.
☐ Listen to complete silence. Shhhhh!

I WILL SURVIVE

276.
☐ Keep a plant alive for a year. Don't forget to water it!

277.
☐ Bake a loaf of bread and enjoy the delicious smell.

278.
☐ Haggle at the market. Don't let yourself be ripped off!

279.
- [ ] Get stung by a (small) jellyfish.
- [ ] It's more painful than an operation without an anaesthetic.
- [ ] I am brave (or at least I pretended to be) and didn't feel a thing.

280.
- [ ] Read the book before the film comes out.
Which was better?
The book/the film.

281.
Buy shares. Are they worth anything?
- [ ] They would pay for a loaf of bread.
(And a jar of chocolate spread, too, with any luck!)
- [ ] They gave me a lovely holiday.
- [ ] I can live off the investments.
Moneybags!

282.
- [ ] Go wild swimming.
Where? _____

283.
☐ Watch a 3D film ☐ without getting a headache.

284.
☐ You are given a surprise party.
☐ I was completely taken by surprise.
☐ I pretended to be surprised because someone had let the cat out of the bag.

285.
☐ Discover your hidden talent.
Which is: _____

_____

286.
☐ Sleep in a castle.
You are a true king/queen.

287. 🎄 Decorate a Christmas tree.

288. ☐ BECOME A MEMBER OF A TEAM OR CLUB.

Maybe the bucket list club! Join us #abucketlistlife

289. ☐ Find Wally!

290. ☐ MAIL A BANANA.
UNWRAPPED, OF COURSE!
LET'S GO BANANAS!

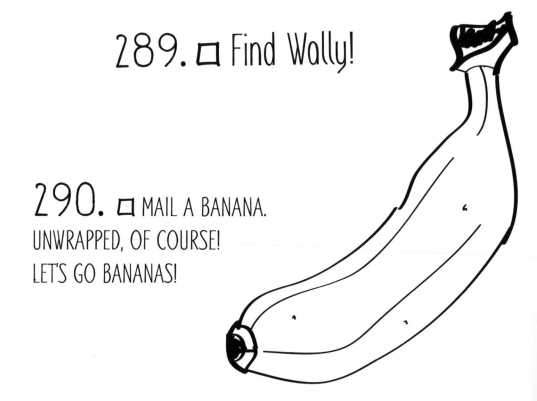

291. ☐ GIVE YOUR CAR A NAME:

_____

DO YOU LIKE IT? THEN GIVE YOUR FURNITURE NAMES, TOO. OR IS THAT TAKING THINGS A BIT TOO FAR?

292. ☐ CATCH A FISH.

293. ☐ Don't throw any food away for a month. Leftovers day, ahem, leftovers month!

294. ☐ Stand in an igloo.

295. ☐ Put one leg behind your head!
(Tip: if you can't do it with your own leg,
do it with somebody else's.)

296. ☐ Attend a funeral.

☐ Spend the night in **297.** hospital.

298.

☐ Pretend you are super-rich in Monaco or St Tropez.
Ask a couple of friends if they'd like to be your bodyguards,
because you need protection!

299.
☐ Appear on television.

Are you ready for your 15 minutes of fame?

300. ☐ Visit a strip club.

301.

☐ Pee standing up.

302.

☐ Write on the walls
of a public toilet.

303.

☐ Leave little notes in library books
for the next reader.

Who wouldn't be delighted?

304.

☐ Keep a diary ☐ about things you
can tick off your bucket list.

305. ☐ Make a note of all your expenses for one month. Every single one! Can you make any savings?

£ _____ £ _____
£ _____ £ _____
£ _____ £ _____
£ _____ £ _____
£ _____ £ _____
£ _____ £ _____
£ _____ £ _____
£ _____ £ _____
£ _____ £ _____
£ _____ £ _____
£ _____ £ _____
£ _____ £ _____
£ _____ £ _____
£ _____ £ _____
£ _____ £ _____
£ _____ £ _____
£ _____ £ _____
£ _____ £ _____
£ _____ £ _____
£ _____ £ _____
£ _____ £ _____
£ _____ £ _____
£ _____ £ _____
£ _____ £ _____
£ _____ £ _____
£ _____
£ _____ TOTAL: £ _____

306.

☐ Be a witness at a wedding.

307.

☐ Get asked to be godmother/godfather of a baby.
What is the little darling's name?_____

308. ☐ Win a medal in _____

You must be very good at it!

309.

☐ Throw a boomerang ☐ and catch it.

310. ■ SPOT THE LOCH NESS MONSTER ■ OR MEET A YETI.

311. ■ DON'T SPEND ANY MONEY FOR A WHOLE WEEK. MONEY CAN'T BUY HAPPINESS!

Although it can help a bit sometimes!

312. ■ ROLL DOWN A HILL.

313. ■ SUFFER JETLAG

Jetlag is a nuisance, but it does mean that you have seen the other side of the world, yay!

314. ☐ Teach something to somebody. Who and what? _____

_____

☐ Choose a random place **315.**
on the map and go there.

Use the map
for number 380!

316.

☐ Be in two countries at the same
time. Which countries?

_____ and _____

317.

☐ Speak the truth and nothing
but the truth for a whole week.

Don't underestimate this challenge: if your girlfriend asks you
if she looks fat in her trousers, give her an honest answer ...

318. ☐ Accept a lift in a car and don't get out until the driver
has reached their destination. Where did you end up?

_____

319. ☐ Eat 10 things you've never eaten before.

- _____
- _____
- _____
- _____
- _____
- _____
- _____
- _____
- _____
- _____

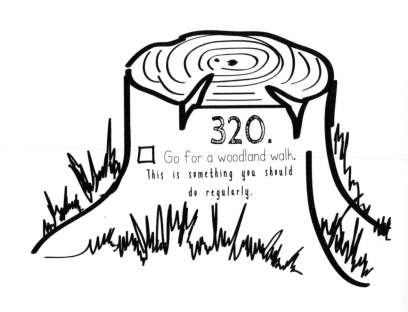

320.
☐ Go for a woodland walk.
This is something you should
do regularly.

321.

☐ Discover your roots (through your family tree) and visit all those countries.

See number 182.

322.

☐ Hold a tarantula (but if just reading this sentence makes you shake, I wish you bon courage).

323.

☐ Go to a psychiatrist and tell them your life history. No secrets!

324.

☐ Walk along the Great Wall of China.

325.

☐ Be part of the audience at a television show (and laugh on cue).

326.

☐ Put money into your pension!

327.

☐ Attend a course. How about dance classes, a photography course or Thai cookery lessons?

328. ☐ Try 25 different modes of transport.

- _____
- _____
- _____
- _____
- _____
- _____
- _____
- _____
- _____
- _____
- _____
- _____
- _____
- _____
- _____
- _____
- _____
- _____
- _____
- _____
- _____
- _____

329.

☐ Fly above the clouds.

Feeling high?

330. ☐ Watch the birth of a baby.

Slide down a ☐ high ☐ water slide **331.**

332. ☐ Do sports twice a week for a year.
Sweat baby, sweat!

Remember: sweat is fat crying.

333.

☐ Apologise to somebody.
Why?

_____

334.

☐ Ring a random telephone number
and sing 'Happy Birthday'.

Happy birthday to you
Happy birthday to you
Happy birthday, dear stranger
Happy birthday to you.

335.

☐ Make a piece of art.

Art is relative, fortunately.

336.

☐ Don't take to heart (or at least not too
seriously) what others think about you.

You're perfect!

337. ☐ Blow a big bubblegum bubble.

Paste a photo of the result here!
(Using bubblegum. Yuck!)

338. ☐ BUILD A SANDCASTLE.

339. ☐ Have a cocktail under a palm tree.

340. ☐
SUMMON SPIRITS.

Be careful, they might really come and spook you!

341. ☐ CATCH A BUTTERFLY.

342.

Visit ☐ Disneyland or ☐ Disneyworld.

It's a whole new world!

343.

☐ Write a letter of complaint and ☐ hope for a freebie.

344.

☐ Go to a restaurant alone! Table for one, please.

345.

☐ Go bungee jumping.

346. ☐ Jump on a bouncy castle. Sometimes being a child again beats everything.

347. ☐ Go to the cinema in your pyjamas. For no reason!

348.

☐ Get brain freeze while eating ice cream.

Probably because you ate five scoops for number 105!

☐ Celebrate a local public holiday in another country. **349.**

350.

☐ Celebrate Chinese New Year and send all your friends a Happy New Year card.

351. ☐ Celebrate your golden wedding anniversary.

Congratulations, it must be true love!

352.

☐ Ask someone to read you a story before you go to sleep.

Trust me, bedtime stories are not just for children!

353.

☐ Record a personal voicemail greeting on your mobile phone. Nothing is as impersonal as 'This is the voicemail of …'.

go outside

AND DO SOMETHING

YOU WILL
REMEMBER

354. ☐ Give your hairdresser carte blanche.

Are you brave enough?

355.

☐ Buy a round of drinks in a pub!

356.

☐ Apply for a job without having the right qualifications

Apply the motto: battles lost are those not fought.

357.

☐ Wear an ushanka hat in Russia.

Google is your friend!

358.

☐ Receive a proposal of marriage or ☐ ask someone to marry you.

359. ☐ Beg until you have received £5.

360. ☐ Visit the Taj Mahal in India.

☐ Catch a fly and set it **361.** free outside.

362.
☐ Watch every film that ever won an Oscar in the 'Best Picture' category. And don't forget to make your own popcorn :-)

363. ☐

WATCH AN ENTIRE SEASON OF A SERIES IN ONE GO.
ADDICTED? YOU? SURELY NOT?

364. ☐ Go to a masked ball
☐ and meet Prince Charming/Cinderella.

365. ☐ Take photos in a photo booth.

↗

Stick the photos here.

366. ☐ Smile at everybody you meet
in the street for a whole day
(or more).

You'll be surprised how people respond.
As if you are mad, which is a shame!

367. ☐ Go to a nudist beach.

368. ☐ BE HOMELESS FOR ONE NIGHT.

369. ☐ Attend an important sports event.

370. ☐ GLUE A POUND COIN TO THE GROUND AND WATCH HOW MANY PEOPLE TRY TO PICK IT UP.

The old ones are the best ones ...

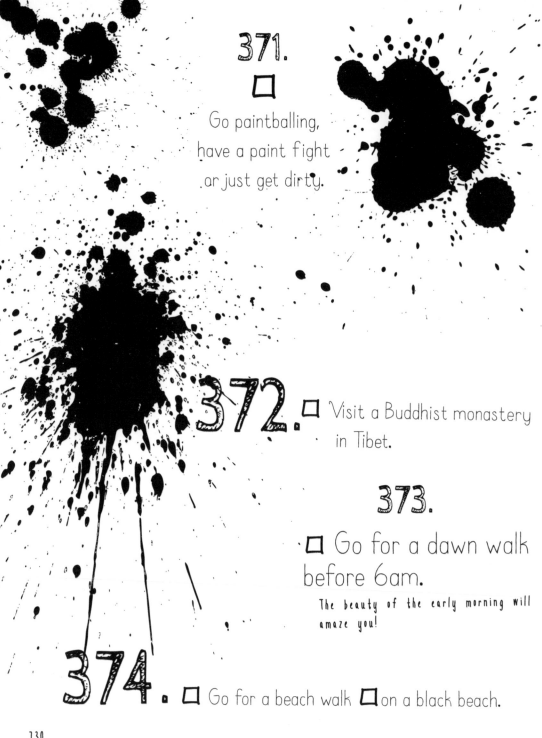

371.
☐
Go paintballing,
have a paint fight
or just get dirty.

372. ☐ Visit a Buddhist monastery in Tibet.

373.

☐ Go for a dawn walk before 6am.
The beauty of the early morning will amaze you!

374. ☐ Go for a beach walk ☐ on a black beach.

375. ☐ Meet a real cowboy.

376. ☐ Ask him to show you how to throw a lasso. Yee-ha!

377. ☐ Watch a caterpillar become a butterfly.

378. ☐ Help an elderly lady cross the road. ↖ GOOD KARMA!

379. ☐ Walk down the red carpet.

380. ☐ MARK ALL THE PLACES YOU HAVE BEEN TO ON THE MAP.

381. ☐ Have a local delicacy in the country of your choice.

What did you eat? _____

382. ☐ Walk on a glacier.

383. ☐ Follow somebody and try to mimic their movements exactly.

384.

☐ Trek through the Amazon.

385. ☐ Ditch a bad habit:

_____

386. ☐ And another one:

_____

387. ☐ Visit 10 sites on the UNESCO World Heritage list.

☐ _____ ☐ _____

☐ _____ ☐ _____

☐ _____ ☐ _____

☐ _____ ☐ _____

☐ _____ ☐ _____

388.

☐ See lightning
and ☐ hear thunder.

389. ☐ Take a monthly photo of your children for 18 years.

They grow up so fast!

☐ Find a word that rhymes with 'orange': **390.**

_____

Let me know if you find one. #abucketlistlife

391.

☐ Ride on an American school bus.

392. ☐ Spread some bizarre gossip at a party to see just how quickly it gets around, but ☐ don't forget to say it was gossip.

393.

☐ Walk the Machu Picchu Inca trail in Peru.

394. ☐ Complete a 3-day detox course.

395. ☐ Have a professional shave at a barber's or ☐ a bikini wax.

396.

☐ Go skating on a frozen lake.

If you fall through a hole in
the ice, tick off number 18.

397. ☐ Stay awake for 24 hours.
Too easy?
☐ Stay awake for 48 hours. Yawn!

398.
☐ Stand on the left ☐ and on
the right of Christ the Saviour
in Brazil.

399. ☐ Eat sushi ☐ in Japan.

400.

☐ Buy a book and have it signed by the author. (Maybe this book?)

I have practised my signature in readiness.

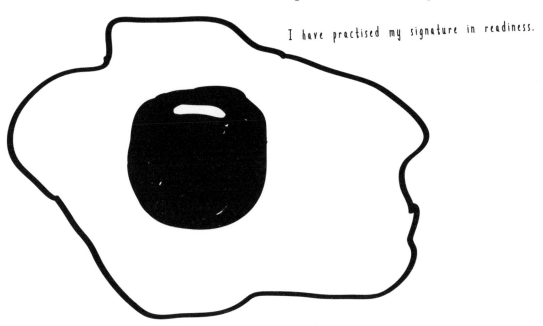

401. ☐ Fry an egg on the bonnet of a car.

402.

☐ Attend a great festival in a foreign country.

403. ☐ Sleep on the Trans-Siberian Railway.

I mean: try to sleep.

404. ☐ SEARCH FOR GOLD ☐ AND FIND IT.

405.
☐ DECLARE YOUR
LOVE TO SOMEONE.

406. ☐ VISIT A ☐ WATER THEME PARK.

407. ☐
Play Twister.

408. ☐ Eat something straight from the tree.

409. ☐ Give a Christmas present to a homeless person.

410. ☐ EAT EACH COURSE OF A 7-COURSE MEAL IN A DIFFERENT RESTAURANT ☐ OR AT DIFFERENT FRIENDS' HOUSES.

411. ☐ HELP A FRIEND IN NEED.

412.

☐ Bury yourself in sand.
(Make sure you keep your head up!)

413.

☐ Wave to the Statue of Liberty
in New York.

414. ☐ Order an unfamiliar dish from a food stall in Bangkok.

415. ☐ Start a new family tradition.
What about giving awards to the best
sister, dearest mother, funniest cousin?

Who will win the award
next year?

416. ☐ Learn something nobody would expect you to and
surprise everybody out of the blue on a random occasion.
(Tip: a backflip, Russian, talking backwards ...)
What is your secret weapon?

- -

417. ☐ Stand on top of the highest building in the world, the Burj Khalifa in Dubai.

418.

☐ Say 'thank you' in the language of each country you have visited.

It's chic to be polite!

419. ☐ Go tornado spotting in Texas.

420. □ Jump out of a cake at a party.

(You MUST stick your evidence here)

421. ☐ Make an important decision by tossing a coin. Heads or tails?

422. ☐ Visit an uninhabited island and ☐ drink milk from a coconut. What would you take with you?

_____

_____

_____

_____

_____

423. ☐ Rescue an animal from a rescue centre.

424. ☐ Visit the Hollywood Walk of Fame. Or even better: ☐ have your own star on the Hollywood Walk of Fame.

Hello Hollywood, are you ready for me?

425.

☐ Cast your vote for the
right party in the elections.

But which is the right one?

426.

☐ Spot a whale in the wild.

427.

☐ Dance at a beach party.

Do you have sand between your toes?

428.

☐ Experience a miracle. Fill me in:

_____

_____

_____

_____

_____

_____

429. ■ Hear your voice on the radio!

430.

■ Don't complain for a whole week and turn all your negative thoughts into positive ones!

431.

■ Meet the ideal man/woman.

432.

■ Hit the bull's-eye with a bow and arrow.

433. □ Say YES to whatever crosses your path all day.

jes Oui Chai avunu Kyllä Áno Hai Evet Diakh Taip Aet Ndiyo ho areh Ya Ndiyo baleh Nai Ja haa'n Taip Po Igen avunu Haa Bœli da Sim Shi Ari tak Weewawo Shi baleh

Have you had to do things you would rather not have done? Spill the beans!

_____

_____

_____

_____

_____

_____

_____

_____

_____

_____

434. ☐ Surprise somebody.

435. ☐ Learn a magic trick
☐ and surprise everyone.

436. ☐ Eat bird's nest soup.

437.
Change the tyre of
☐ a car ☐ a bicycle.

Clever you! Now carry on with your journey.

438. ☐ Go on a road trip without a destination.

439. ☐ Make someone change their mind on a subject after you discuss it with them.

440. ☐ Donate your hair to a good cause!

This is a difficult thing to do and you should only do so if you really want to. But knowing that it will make a cancer patient very happy might make the decision a little less difficult.

441.

☐ Have yourself dropped off in an unfamiliar location and find your way home.
PS: You are not allowed to have any money on you. Be creative!

442. ☐ Go to a gig by a singer or band you have never heard before.

Everybody deserves a chance, don't they?

Doing

IS WHAT MAKES A

DREAM
COME TRUE

443. ☐ Visit Niagara Falls.

You might be able to tick number 103 jere, too.

444. ☐ RELEASE A HELIUM BALLOON WITH A MESSAGE FOR THE FINDER.

445.

☐ KISS SOMEBODY UNDER THE MISTLETOE.

446. ☐ Laugh until you cry and your tummy muscles hurt.

447. ☐ Go for a medical check-up.

448.
☐ Lay flowers on a
neglected grave.

449. ☐ MAKE SOMETHING OF YOUR LIFE.

450. ☐ MAKE A SNOW ANGEL.

If you don't know how:
lie on your back in the snow and move your
arms up and down a couple of times.

451.

☐ Enjoy an extremely luxurious day.

Yes please!

452.

☐ Jump off a cliff into water.

453.

☐ Learn (one sentence in) sign language.

454.

☐ Sleep in a hammock.

Be a lazybones!

455.

☐ Go on a (hitch-hiking) holiday with only £200 on you.

456.

☐ Eat candyfloss on a Ferris wheel.

457.

☐ See a corpse.

Or maybe you'd rather not!

458.

☐ Help someone who is seriously ill.

459. ☐ LEARN THE ORIGINS OF ALL THE FEAST DAYS.

☐ Smell the lavender fields in Provence. **460.**

461. ☐ Live abroad for 3 months (or longer)!

462.
☐ Swim in the sea at night.

463. ☐ Have a family portrait taken.

464.

☐ Checkmate
someone in a
game of chess.

□ Jump out of a plane. **465.**

466.
□ Fantasise about what you would do
if you won the lottery.

It's best to be prepared!

467.
☐ Complete an entire crossword.

468.

☐ Hide a £50 note in your winter coat when you put it away for the summer.

It will be fun to find all that money six months later!

☐ Close your eyes, point at a dish in a restaurant and order that meal.

469.

470.
☐ Make 20 sincere compliments per day for a whole week.

471. ☐ Touch your toes with your legs straight.

472. ☐ Walk in high heels.

☐ Learn to write with your left hand. **473.**

(Or your right hand if you're left-handed.)

474.

☐ Coat yourself in sunblock cream on every sunny day, even in winter.

475.
☐ Have a look behind the scenes in a brewery, chocolate factory, or other venue that interests you.

476.
☐ Go surfing. (Or try.)

477.
☐ Don't drink alcohol for a whole month.

If you find it difficult, you might have a problem.

478.
☐ Spend 24 hours in a wheelchair
☐ and find out how terribly annoying all those bumps in the street can be.

479.

☐ Meet someone who shares your name.
First name and family name! Unless you are
called Shaniqua-Belle Delomoreo (or have another
unusual name).

☐ Try acupuncture. # 480.

I hope you are not afraid of needles!

481.

☐ Eat spaghetti like the   Lady and the Tramp.
Slurp

482.

☐ Write a letter to a random
address and ☐ hope they reply.

Open a telephone directory, point at a name, and that's
your recipient! Don't forget to stick on a stamp.

483. ☐ ORGANISE A GREAT PARTY AND BE THE CENTRE OF ATTENTION THAT WHOLE DAY! IT'S ALL ABOUT YOU!

484. ☐ GET IN'VITED TO A PREMIERE.

485. ☐ Do some voluntary work!

486. ☐ MAKE A BEST FRIEND. BECAUSE REAL FRIENDS MAKE THOSE FUN MOMENTS EVEN BETTER AND DIFFICULT TIMES EASIER!

481. ☐ Buy tulips in Amsterdam.

~~Wish~~ do

488. ☐ Sleep on the beach!

489. ☐ Receive or ☐ give away a teddy bear
at a funfair.

490. ☐ HAVE A ROW ☐ AND MAKE UP
AGAIN.

491. ☐ Write something here with a quill and ink.

492. ☐ Fall asleep and ☐ wake up again beside the love of your life.

493.

☐ Put your foot in it, literally!
What was it you put your foot in?

494.
☐ Wet your pants.
(Maybe you can tick this straight away?)

495.

☐ Watch all 10 seasons of Friends.

If you have not yet been able to tick 363, you might be able to do so now.

496.

☐ Go on holiday with friends.

497.
☐ Observe penguins in their natural habitat. *Happyfeet*

498.

☐ Grow your own vegetables.

Or don't you have green fingers?

499. ☐ AIM FOR HEALTHY AGEING!

500.

TICK ALL THE ITEMS
IN THIS BOOK.

5 TIPS FOR YOUR BUCKET LIST

1. Write down your bucket list. By putting your dreams on paper, you are more likely to make them come true. You are making a promise to yourself. *pinkyswear*. This book has 500 suggestions, but you are sure to have other dreams, too. The following pages are meant for all your personal wishes and goals. (Dream big)

2. Go for variety. Make sure that your list offers a good balance of smaller and bigger challenges. The easy items will boost your motivation to achieve the more difficult ones. Give yourself enough variety across these six categories: experiences, travel/culture, body/health, knowledge/skills, love/friendship/family, and so on.

3. Remain motivated! There is nothing to prevent you from making hundreds of lists, but if you never read them, what's the point? Sound familiar? Try to go down your bucket list every month and tick something off regularly.

4. Share your experiences and be inspired by others! By sharing your bucket list with friends and family (why not with the rest of the world?) you will inspire them to create an action plan and help yourself to keep ticking off as many items as you can. You don't want others to think you're a quitter, do you?
#abucketlistlife

5. Enjoy! This is undoubtedly the most valuable tip that can be given to you. ENJOY THE RIDE!

- [ ] _____
- [ ] _____
- [ ] _____
- [ ] _____
- [ ] _____
- [ ] _____
- [ ] _____
- [ ] _____
- [ ] _____
- [ ] _____
- [ ] _____
- [ ] _____
- [ ] _____
- [ ] _____
- [ ] _____
- [ ] _____
- [ ] _____
- [ ] _____
- [ ] _____
- [ ] _____

<------ DREAMERS

Your road to happiness starts here!

▫ ▫ ▫ ▫ ▫ ▫ ▫ ▫ ▫ ▫ ▫ ▫ ▫

▫ ▫ ▫ ▫ ▫ ▫ ▫ ▫ ▫ ▫ ▫ ▫ ▫ ▫ ▫ ▫▫ ▫ ▫

▫ ▫ ▫ ▫ ▫ ▫ ▫ ▫ ▫ ▫▫ ▫ ▫ ▫ ▫ ▫ ▫ ▫ ▫ ▫

100 dreams became 100 beautiful
memories, so cherish them!

▫ ▫ ▫ ▫ ▫ ▫ ▫ ▫ ▫ ▫ ▫ ▫ ▫

▫ ▫ ▫ ▫ ▫ ▫ ▫ ▫ ▫ ▫ ▫ ▫ ▫ ▫ ▫ ▫ ▫ ▫ ▫ ▫

▫ ▫ ▫ ▫ ▫ ▫ ▫ ▫ ▫ ▫ ▫ ▫ ▫ ▫ ▫ ▫ ▫ ▫ ▫ ▫

▫ ▫ ▫ ▫ ▫ ▫ ▫ ▫ ▫ ▫ ▫ ▫ ▫ ▫ ▫ ▫ ▫ ▫ ▫ ▫

Halfway there! How does it feel? ▫ ▫ ▫ ▫ ▫ ▫▫ ▫ ▫ ▫ ▫ ▫ ▫ ▫

▫ ▫ ▫ ▫ ▫ ▫ ▫ ▫ ▫ ▫ ▫ ▫ ▫ ▫▫ ▫ ▫ ▫ ▫ ▫

▫ ▫ ▫ ▫ ▫ ▫ ▫ ▫ ▫ ▫ ▫ ▫ ▫ ▫ ▫ ▫ ▫ ▫ ▫

▫ ▫ ▫ ▫ ▫ ▫ ▫ ▫ ▫ ▫ ▫ ▫ ▫ ▫ ▫ ▫ ▫ ▫ ▫

▫ ▫ ▫ ▫ ▫ Another 100 dreams to go! ▫ ▫ ▫ ▫ ▫ ▫ ▫ ▫
            You're doing so well!

▫ ▫ ▫ ▫ ▫ ▫ ▫ ▫ ▫ ▫ ▫ ▫ ▫ ▫ ▫ ▫ ▫ ▫ ▫

▫ ▫ ▫ ▫ ▫ ▫ ▫ ▫ ▫ ▫ ▫ ▫ ▫ ▫ ▫ ▫ ▫ ▫ ▫

ARE YOU A DREAMER OR A GO-GETTER?

You can monitor your progress on this page. It will be particularly useful for when you need motivation! Has it been a while since you filled in a square? Try to tick a simple item on the list!

□ □

Wow, your first 50 dreams have now been realised. Are you ready to continue?

□ □ □ □ □ □ □ □ □ □ □

□ □ □ □ □ □ □ □ □ □ □ □ □ □ □ □

□ □ □ □ □ □ □ □ □ □ □ □ □ □ □ □ □ □

□ □ □ □ □ □ □ □ □ □ □ □ □ □ □ □ □ □ □

□ □ □ □ □ □ □ □ □ □ □ □ □ □ □ □ □ □ □

□ □ □ □ □ □ □ □ □ □ □ □ □ □ □ □ □ □ □ □

□ □ □ □ □ □ □ □ □ □ □ □ □ □ □ □ □ □ □ □

□ □ □ □ □ □ □ □ □ □ □ □ □ □ □ □ □ □

□ □ □ □ □ □ □ □ □ □ □ □ □ □ □ □ □ □ □

□ □ □ □ □ □ □ □ □ □ □ □ □ □ □ □ □ □ □

□ □ □ □ □ □ □ □ □ □ □ □ □ □ □ □ □ □ □

□ □ □ □ □ □ □ □ □ □ □ □ □ □ □ □ □ □ □

□ □ □

500! But don't worry, there's still so much left to be discovered, even for you!

GO-GETTERS ----->

First published in the United Kingdom in 2018 by
Portico
43 Great Ormond Street
London
WC1N 3HZ
An imprint of Pavilion Books Company Ltd

First published in Belgium in 2015 by Uitgeverij Lannoo
© Uitgeverij Lannoo, 2015
Text: Elise de Rijck
Design: Valérie Machtelinckx in collaboration with Elise De Rijck

ISBN 978-1-91162-208-6

A CIP catalogue record for this book is available from the British Library.

10 9 8 7 6 5 4 3 2 1

Reproduction by Mission Productions Ltd, Hong Kong
Printed and bound in China by 1010 Printing International Limited

This book can be ordered direct from the publisher at www.pavilionbooks.com